LaFayette Stiles Pence

A History of the Kentucky and Missouri Stiles

LaFayette Stiles Pence

A History of the Kentucky and Missouri Stiles

ISBN/EAN: 9783741187612

Manufactured in Europe, USA, Canada, Australia, Japa

Cover: Foto ©ninafisch / pixelio.de

Manufactured and distributed by brebook publishing software
(www.brebook.com)

LaFayette Stiles Pence

A History of the Kentucky and Missouri Stiles

A HISTORY

OF THE

Kentucky and Missouri

STILES,

WITH A

Sketch of New Jersey and Other Kindred.

BY
LaFayette Stiles Pence.

LEBANON, KENTUCKY.
W. T. HAWKINS, BOOK AND JOB PRINTER.
1896.

PREFACE.

THIS Little Book gives the history and recollections of the Stiles family in Kentucky and Missouri.
While it is not as lengthy as desired, only spare moments have been devoted to it. Beginning at the earliest date I was able to find, I have come down the line, aiming to keep each division separate, that the reader may be able to trace his or her branch of the family.

Portraits of a few have been added with impartial estimates as from personal, or other knowledge. I felt justified in making.

Letters from the New Jersey and other kinspeople I have inserted. These letters were found among my grandfather's papers only a short while ago. These may prove interesting to the descendants of these generous and warm-hearted contributors. These letters bear tidings from the writers that here once lived kindred they admired and cherished and wrote to so encouragingly and kindly. Will say, very earnestly and cordially, that I would appreciate the favor to know the descendants of these kindred, not only by the mention of their names in this book, but personally. With great esteem to all,

Yours Most Sincerely,

THE AUTHOR.

LEBANON, KY., March, 1896.

FIRST DIVISION.

THE Stiles herein mentioned are descendants of New Jersey and Connecticut families of that name. The earliest one to come to Kentucky was David Stiles.

David Stiles was a son of Thomas and Abagail Ogden Stiles; was born in 1760 near Morristown, N. J. David's grandfather (Thomas' father) was "Long" Jonathan Stiles, who was born about 1688 in Stratford, Conn., and came to Morristown, N. J., in about 1730; died about 1758. "Long" Jonathan Stiles married (1) Rebecca Canfield, (2) Elizabeth Taylor. Thomas (David's father) was issue of the last marriage. Thomas Stiles died in or near Morristown, N. J., in about 1802. By a record in my possession, administration on his estate was granted to his son, David, in April, 1803.

David Stiles came to Kentucky in 1809, settling near the Rolling Fork river, eighteen miles from Bardstown, in Nelson County. David left only one brother in New Jersey, Jacob Stiles, who was born in 1764. Jacob Stiles went to Bridport, Vt., from Morristown, N. J., soon after his brother, David, left Morristown for Kentucky.

Jacob Stiles married Polly Johnson. No children. He died in Bridport on Aug. 28, 1847, and his wife died Aug. 27, 1847, twenty-five hours apart. Both were buried in the same grave, and a well constructed monument marks their resting place in Bridport (Vt.) Cemetery.

David and Jacob Stiles had four sisters, viz. :

Elizabeth Stiles,	b. 1761,	d. 1841,	mar.	Abraham Losey.
Rhoda Stiles,		" 1828,	"	Ezekiel Munson.
Mary Stiles,		" 1830,	"	Moses Hurd.
Sally Stiles,		" 1847,	"	Jonathan Ball.

David Stiles married Elizabeth Kitchell, daughter of Abraham and Charity Ford Kitchell, in New Jersey, about 1784. He died in Nelson County, Ky., December, 1839, eight years after the death of his wife.

These are the children of David and Elizabeth Stiles (all born in New Jersey).

Lewis Stiles,	b. 1785,	d. 1858.
Charles Stiles,	" 1788,	" 1872.
Eunice Kitchell Stiles,	" 1792,	" 1879.
Densy Stiles,	" 1794,	" 1866.
John Stiles,	" 1796,	" 1876.
Chillion Stiles,	" 1798,	" 1878.
Rhoda Stiles,	" 1800,	" 1888.
Abraham Stiles,	" 1802.	
Demas Stiles,	" 1805.	" 1870.
David Stiles,	" 1807,	" 1875.

Joseph Kitchell Stiles (died young).

David Stiles' Sons and Daughters and Their Children.

LEWIS STILES.

Lewis Stiles was born Sept. 13, 1785, near Morristown, N. J., and when twenty-four years of age came with his father (David) to Kentucky. He attained an education only at the county schools of his native

Capt. Lewis Stiles.

State. At the age of twenty-nine years he was commissioned [1] a Lieutenant and [2] Captain in the War of 1812, by Gov. Isaac Shelby, Kentucky's first Governor. He was a Magistrate, by appointment, of his county for many years; was appointed Postmaster at Rolling Fork, Ky., in 1824. He held many times the office of executor and guardian of many trusts, which he administered with fidelity and satisfaction. He choose to avoid public station and confined himself to the legitimate phases of agriculture. He was a large land owner and distiller.

Lewis Stiles married Rebecca Willett, Sept. 22, 1814. Issue:

Susan Ann Stiles,	b. Sept. 3, 1815,	d. Oct. 16, 1858.
Mary Elizabeth Stiles,	" Nov. 9, 1817,	" Oct. 15, 1887.
Kitchell Mathias Stiles,	" Sept. 16, 1819,	" Aug. 27, 1885.
Sarah Jane Stiles,	" Nov. 1, 1821,	" June 21, 1880.
Ogden Willett Stiles,	" Dec. 7, 1823,	" July 28, 1878.
Caroline Stiles,	" Sept. 28, 1826,	" April 16, 1864.
La Fayette Stiles,	" Nov. 30, 1828.	
Minerva Ford Stiles,	} " Jan. 30, 1831.	
Rebecca Eltengy Stiles	" Jan. 30, 1831,	" Oct. 27, 1867.
Martha Ellen Stiles,	" April 27, 1833,	" July 11, 1880.
Martin Van Buren Stiles,	" Sept. 9, 1835.	

CHARLES STILES.

Charles Stiles was born in New Jersey on the 14th day of May, 1788; died the 6th day of October, 1872; married to Mary Willett. Issue:

Abraham Stiles,	b. 1822,	d. 1890,	mar.	—— Thomas.
Mary Ann Stiles,	" 1825,		"	Charles Beeler.
Rebecca Eltengy Stiles,	" 1827,	" 1888,	"	H.L. Pottenger.
Lewis Fisk Stiles,	" 1829,		"	—— Thomas.
Emily Jane Stiles,	" 1836,	" 1865,	"	— Hazelwood.
Rev. Jacob W. Stiles,	" 1838,		"	—— Beeler.

Christy Ann Stiles,   " 1840,   " John T. Gaddie.
Charles Stiles,   " 1842, " 1865.

Charles Stiles was a generous-hearted, public-spirited man, and his duties were marked with firmness and fidelity. He lived a consecrated life, was a consistent member of the Methodist Church.

EUNICE KITCHELL STILES.

Eunice Kitchell Stiles, born February, 1792, in New Jersey; married to Joe Maxwell in 1814; died in December, 1879. Joe Maxwell was going out with a cargo on a flat-boat in the Rolling Fork river, when his boat came in contact with a tree that had fallen in the river near David Stiles' house. He went to the house to get an ax with which to clear away the tree, and there saw Eunice at the spinning wheel. He was much smitten with her, visited and married her after two years' courtship. Issue:

David Stiles Maxwell, b. 1815, d. 1885.
John Cleland Maxwell,   " 1816,   " 1895.
Hugh Hall Maxwell,   " 1818,   " ——
James Maxwell,   " 1821,   " 1858, mar. (1) Everhart.
                                          " (2) Grundy.
Julia Etta Maxwell,   " 1822,   " 1894, " W. L. Tarkington
Mary Eliza Maxwell,   " ——   " ——   " (1) Cowherd.
                                          " (2) McMillen.
Mattie Maxwell,   " 1828,   " 1884, " David Knox.
Sarah Jane Maxwell,   " 1831,   " 1878, " Thos. McElroy.
Lettie Maxwell,   " 1836,   " 1894, " James Harlan.

I must especially mention Dr. J. C. Maxwell, for he was one of the best men I ever knew. He was a Post Surgeon in the United States Army and a man of high standing and command during the war. His honesty of purpose and worth as a man showed him to be a

Charles Stiles.

just and generous man towards all alike. No man was better known or more universally beloved in Central Kentucky than Dr. Maxwell. In his church work (Northern Presbyterian) he was an active and faithful member. He married [1] Emily B. Howell and [2] Ellen Doneghy. His only child, Emma, by first wife, married D. H. Howard, who was Deputy Collector of Fifth District of Kentucky for over twenty years. D. H. and Emma Howard have two bright and beautiful daughters, Emogene and Juliet, and three sons, Maxwell, Lucius and Ward.

DENSY STILES.

Densy Stiles, born in New Jersey, Jan. 27, 1794; married to Jessie Phillips; died Dec. 31, 1866. Issue:

James F. Phillips,	b. July 13, 1812,	d. 1864.		
David B. Phillips,	" Mar. 15, 1821,			mar. Vertrees.
Elizabeth M. Phillips,	" Apr. 17, 1823,	" 1854,	"	Miller.
Charles P. Phillips,	" Nov. 11, 1824.			(In Missouri.)
William Phillips,	" Sept. 15, 1827,	" 1859.		
Martha A. Phillips,	" Sept. 26, 1829,	" 1854,		" Starks.

JOHN STILES.

John Stiles, born in New Jersey, Sept. 6, 1796. On Sept. 5, 1822, he was married to Rhoda Edwards; died Sept. 19, 1876. Issue:

James Ford Stiles,	b. 1823.		(Bachelor.)
Eunice Stiles,	" 1824,	d. 1890,	mar. Jacob A. Miller.
Elizabeth Stiles,	" 1826,	" 1839.	
Thomas Stiles,	" 1828,	" 1862.	
John Calvin Stiles,	" 1830,		" Elizabeth Carter.
Henry Stiles,	" 1832,		" Bettie Uptegrove.
Jacob Stiles,	" 1834,	" 1835.	
Electa Stiles,	" 1835,		" Thomas Starks.

Joseph Stiles,   " 1838,   " 1838.
David Thomas Stiles, " 1840,   " 1862.
Demas Stiles,   " 1842,   " Lucy Phillips.
Jonathan Stiles,   " 1844,   " Lizzie Coakley.
Sallie Stiles,   " 1850,   " Lafe Stiles.

Jonathan Stiles lives upon the "Old David Stiles' Home-place," a farm of some 320 acres, most of it fertile bottom land. The house erected by David Stiles burned some twelve or fifteen years ago, destroying many pictures of the New Jersey relatives and all the old family letters.

CHILLION STILES.

Chillion Stiles, born in New Jersey in 1798; died in Kentucky in 1878; married to Elizabeth Miller. Issue:

Cleland Stiles,   b. 1827,   mar. Redman.
Jane Stiles,   " 1843, d. 1892,   " Dr. W. T. Lively.
Mary Ann Stiles, " ——   " ——
Arabella Stiles,   " ——   " accident,   " Underwood.

RHODA STILES.

Rhoda Stiles was born in New Jersey in March, 1800; married to Griffin Willett in 1818; died Dec. 20, 1888. Issue:

Elizabeth Willett,   b. 1820,   d. —   mar. J. McDougal.
Corilla Willett,   " 1822,   " Elijah H. Bland.
Darius Willett,   " 1824,   " —   " (1) Carter (2) Kirtley.
Mahulda Willett,   " 1827,   " —   " Robert Sanders.
George Willett,   " 1829,   " —   " (1) Newlan (2) Rush.
Dr. Franklin Willett, " 1832,   " —   " Bland.
David Munson Willett " 1835,   " Duana M. Beeler.
Margaret Ann Willett " 1837,   " John G. Gaddie.

This Rhoda was a namesake of Rhoda Stiles of New

Jersey, who married Ezekiel Munson. Regret I can not find a photograph of this woman. She often related incidents of her childhood days in "Jersey."

ABRAHAM STILES.

Abraham Stiles was born in New Jersey in 1802; married (1) Ferriell and (2) Dye; died about 1856. Issue:

Franklin Stiles,	b. 1836,	mar.	Ellen Martin.
Mary Elizabeth Stiles,	" 1838,	"	George Charlton.
Densy Stiles,	" 1840,	"	Jas. Smith.
Eunice Stiles,	" 1842,	"	John Allison.
Maxwell Stiles,	" 1844,	"	Susan Neff.
Ambrose Denton Stiles.	" 1846,	"	Mollie Neff.

DEMAS STILES.

Demas Stiles was born in New Jersey, January, 1805; married (1) Margaret Ann Owsley, of Kentucky, in 1827. Resided in Kentucky until 1832, moved to Johnson County, Mo., and died there Dec. 7, 1870. Issue:

David Thomas Stiles,	b. 1829,		mar. Mary L. Bell.
Henry Mason Stiles,	" 1831,	d. 1851,	in California.
Nancy Stiles,	" 1834,		" Henry Cooper.
John Lewis Stiles,	" 1837,	" in Southern Army.	
William Kitchell Stiles,	" 1842.		

Demas Stiles married (2) Tamson Bazzill. Issue:

James Riley Stiles,	b. 1847,	mar.	Mary M. Jackson.
Francis Marion Stiles,	" 1850, dead.		
Charles Cleland, Stiles,	" 1852,	"	Jerusha Ann Slayden.
Mary Alice Stiles,	" 1853,	"	Henry Jackson.
Arabella Stiles,	" 1855,	"	Wm. B. Doyal.
Sallie Audoxia Stiles,	" 1856,	"	Wm. R. Duckworth.
Eliza Jane Stiles,	" 1858,	"	Thomas J. Ellis.
George Franklin Stiles,	" 1861,	"	Ora B. Butcher.

The Missouri Branch of the Stiles has David Stiles, of Kentucky, as ancestor. This family is not well enough known to Kentucky Branch as it should be. Hope this may be the means of letting one another be better known.

Miss Jennie L. Stiles made a visit, in September, 1895, to many of the Kentucky Stiles, the first one to visit the "old homestead" of her foreparents.

DAVID STILES, JR.

David Stiles, Jr., was born Feb. 14, 1807; married [1] Goodman; died May 3, 1875. Issue:

Somira Stiles,   b. 1844,   d. 1895,   mar. Shipley.
Minerva Stiles.

David Stiles, Jr., married [2] Daugherty. Issue:

Annie Stiles,	b. 1840,	mar.	Smith.
Elizabeth Stiles,	" 1842,	"	Miller.
Charles Stiles,	" 1845,	"	Neff.
William Stiles,	" 1847,	"	Harnett.
John Francis Stiles,	" 1849,	"	Loving.
Thomas Lewis Stiles,	" 1852,	"	(1) Scott, (2) Godbey.
Sallie E. Stiles,	" 1854,	"	Williams.

NOTE.—Charles Stiles married Nancy Willett. It should read Nancy instead of Mary, on page 5.

Mary Elizabeth Phillips.

SECOND DIVISION.

Lewis Stiles' Sons and Daughters and Their Children.

SUSAN ANN STILES.

Susan Ann Stiles married (1) Martin Ray. Issue:
Lewis Martin Ray, in Texas.

Susan Ann Stiles married (2) Wash Thomas. Issue:

Susan Thomas,   mar. Ike Reynolds.
Carrie Thomas,   "   Melton.
Latimer Thomas, dead.
John Thomas.   " .
Wash Thomas, Jr.   "

MARY ELIZABETH STILES.

Mary Elizabeth Stiles married (1) George Ray and (2) Sam Phillips. Issue:
Rebecca J. Ray, b. 1839, d. 1894, mar. Alfred G. Nall.

Mary E. Phillips was a type of true Kentucky womanhood, and her life was spent in usefulness and for gracious influences. The mother of one child, this daughter married A. G. Nall, the noted distiller. Rebecca Nall was endowed richly with natural gifts and graces. She was a friend to all that needed her friendship. She left four sons, Jas. R., George C., William and Burr, and two daughters, Mary Phillips and Carrie Nall.

KITCHELL MATHIAS STILES.

Kitchell Mathias Stiles married Caroline Hobbs. Issue:

Lewis Ogden Stiles, b. 1855, mar. Nannie Chenault.
Annie Stiles,   " 1859,   " John P. Collins.
Mary Stiles,   " Dr. E. S. Smith.
Rebecca Stiles,   " Tarpley.

This man was a namesake of Mathias Kitchell, of New Jersey. He was a scholarly, saintly man; his loyalty to those he loved was without limit.

SARAH J. STILES.

Sarah J. Stiles married Thomas J. Beall. Issue:

Stiles Washington Beall, b. 1843, d. 1866. Served under Gen. John Morgan, C.S.A.
Mary E. Beall,   " 1848, mar. Dr. H. B. Peterson.
George E. Beall,   " 1853,   " Annie Williams.
Sam P. Beall,   " 1856.   " Sudie Schooling.
Thomas J. Beall,   " 1858,   " Maggie Beeler.

Lewis Stiles, in his diary for the year 1842, says: "Sarah Jane married 14th of April; 62 youngsters were her company, the same accompanied her to her father's-in-law, Washington Beall; two of the finest wedding days imaginable." Mary E., her only daughter, has two sons, Stiles Tolbert and Wesley W., and a daughter, Annie B. Peterson, who married William Webster, Dec. 11, 1895.

OGDEN WILLET STILES.

Ogden Willett Stiles married [1] Lizzie Phillips. Issue:

Rev. Sam Phillips Stiles, b. 1848. Ministry M. E. Church South, mar. Annie Huston.
Lewis Kitchell Stiles, b. 1850, mar. Kate Huston.

Ogden Willett Stiles married [2] Susan Beckham. Issue:

Ogden Willett Stiles.

John Breckinridge Stiles, b. 1856, d. 1890, mar. Sallie Beam.
Ben Piles Stiles, " 1862, " Lena Elliott.
Hugh Dunlap Stiles, " 1864, " Woodie Crume.

To his friends he was kind and true, and no favor asked, great or small, was ever refused. He never did any human being knowingly a wrong.

Uncle "Ogden," as he was called, was fond of the little folks.

CAROLINE STILES.

Caroline Stiles married George Schooling. Issue:
Susan Ray Schooling, b. 1852, mar. Sam P. Beall.

LAFAYETTE STILES.

La Fayette Stiles married Sallie Stiles. Issue:
Rhoda Stiles, b. (about) 1877.
Rebecca Stiles.
La Fayette Stiles.
Mattie Stiles.
John Cleveland Stiles.

The writer's namesake. A prosperous farmer of Nelson County. For many years he and his brother, V. B. Stiles, and brother-in-law, G. W. Beall, operated (after building) the distillery now known in Kentucky as "Newcomb-Buchanan Co.," in Louisville. In politics an "out and out" Democrat, but no semblance of a politician.

MINERVA FORD STILES.

Minerva Ford Stiles married George W. Beall. Issue:
Lizzie Laura Beall (died young).
Mary Mattie Beall, b. 1856, mar. Joe N. Wilson.

When the writer's mother died, October, 1867, he was left in the care and keeping of Minerva and George Beall. No language of mine can express due appreciation of their loving kindness.

George Washington Beall, born 1825, was a son of Washington Beall, who belonged to that old generation in Maryland, and who came to Kentucky in early days. G. W. Beall was the head of the noted distillery firm of "Beall, Stiles & Co." in Louisville, soon after the war and when that business was on a paying basis in this State. He is at present engaged in farming on four splendid farms in Marion County.

Their daughter, Mattie Wilson, has two children, Margaret Beall, a bright and rosy girl of five years, and George Beall, aged one year, a great boy he is.

REBECCA ELTENGY STILES.

Rebecca Eltengy Stiles married John W. Pence. Issue:

William Lewis Pence,	b. 1855.	In Missouri.
Caroline M. Pence,	" 1858.	
Sarah Pence,	" 1860,	mar. Will Wright.
Mary Phillips Pence,	" 1862, d. 1892,	" Atkin Beeler.

"There's a land where those we loved while here shall meet to love again."

A fond mother passed to her reward on Oct. 27, 1867.

LAFAYETTE STILES PENCE.

MARTHA ELLEN STILES.

Martha Ellen Stiles was never married. She was in quick and strong sympathy with every good work, and was willing to assist with her own hands and her means. She died July 11, 1880.

Caroline Schooling.

MARTIN VANBUREN STILES.

Martin Vanburen Stiles married Annie Bland. Issue:

Joseph Bland Stiles,	b. 1875,	d. 1888.
George F. Stiles,	" 1876,	" 1878.
Lewis Kitchell Stiles,	" 1880.	
Elijah Bland Stiles,	" 1883.	
Corilla Pearl Stiles,	" 1885.	
Roy Ogden Stiles,	" 1890.	

He is a pushing, thriving farmer, and has some splendid farms. He is growing in wealth and influence yearly.

Charles Stiles' Sons and Their Children.

NOTE.—I shall only mention children of the sons. It is impossible to furnish them of all. Many of the sons whose children bear the name direct will not furnish a list of their own family. AUTHOR.

LEWIS FISK STILES.

Lewis Fisk Stiles married —— Thomas. No information furnished. Resides somewhere in Southern Kentucky.

REV. JACOB W. STILES.

Rev. Jacob W. Stiles, Ministry Baptist Church, married —— Beeler. Issue:

Maggie Stiles,	b. 1865,	mar.	Thomas.
Charles Stiles,	" 1867,	"	Brown.
Emma Stiles,	" 1868.		
Carrie Stiles.			
Rebecca Stiles,		"	R. Beeler.
James Stiles.			
Robert Stiles.			
Vaughn Stiles.			

John Stiles' Sons and Their Children.

JOHN CALVIN STILES.

John Calvin Stiles married Elizabeth Carter. Issue:
David Thomas Stiles, b. 1864, mar. Bettie Miller.
Edward J. Stiles.
John Calvin Stiles.
Mary R. Stiles.
James Ford Stiles.
Burr H. Stiles.
Charles G. Stiles.
Chillion H. Stiles.

HENRY STILES.

Henry Stiles married Elizabeth Uptegrove. Issue:
Jennie Lee Stiles.

Chillion Stiles' Son and His Children.

CLELAND STILES.

Cleland Stiles married —— Redmon. Issue:

Thomas Stiles,	b. 1852,	d. 1891.		
Helen Stiles,		" young.		
Elias Stiles,	" 1857,		mar.	Wade.
Chillion Stiles,	" 1859,		"	Tandy.
Maggie Stiles,	" 1861,		"	Young.
Elizabeth Stiles,		" young.		
John Stiles,	" 1865,	" ——	"	McFarran.
Lida Stiles,	" 1867,			

Abraham Stiles Sons and Their Children.

MAXWELL STILES.

Maxwell Stiles (dead) married Susan Neff.

David Thomas Stiles, Windsor, Mo.

AMBROSE STILES.

Ambrose Stiles married Mollie Neff. Issue:
Maxwell Stiles.
Carl Stiles.

Demas Stiles' Sons and Their Children.

DAVID THOMAS STILES.

David Thomas Stiles married [1] Mary Geary. Issue:
Melissa Margaret Stiles.
William Henry Stiles.

David Thomas Stiles married [2] Nancy L. Bell. Issue:
Isabella Stiles.
David Lewis Stiles.
Jennie Lee Stiles.

David Thomas Stiles was born in Hardin Co., (now Larue), Ky., Sept. 21, 1829. In 1839 he went to Missouri with his father, settled on an open prairie, but where now the charming town of Windsor stands. He and his brother Henry went to California in 1848 to seek their fortune in mines. In 1852 he returned home by way of the Isthmus of Panama. Henry died in California. On Aug. 10, 1862, he joined the Southern Army under Cockrell's command, and was in some of the hottest battles fought. He was transferred to Gen. Price's command, and at Shreveport the Commander surrendered.

From Shreveport he set sail for home on the steamboat "Old Kentucky," which sank in Red river. He was among the survivors and finally reached home in Johnson County, where he has since resided, being a successful and enterprising farmer and stock raiser. In 1892 he retired from active business and removed with his family to Windsor. He is a zealous member of the Baptist Church and has been for thirty-eight years.

DEMAS STILES, JR.

Demas Stiles, Jr., married Eliza Doyal. Issue:

Charles Stiles.
Nannie Lee Stiles.
Josie Isabelle Stiles.
Lida May Stiles.
Hugh Demas Stiles.

GEORGE FRANKLIN STILES.

George Franklin Stiles married Ora B. Butcher. Issue:

Frank Stiles.
Nora Evaline Stiles.

JAMES RILEY STILES.

James Riley Stiles married Mary Milvin Jackson. Issue:

James Stiles.
Lizzie M. Stiles.

CHARLES CLELAND STILES.

Charles Cleland Stiles married Jerusha A. Slayden. No issue given.

WM. KITCHELL STILES.

Wm. Kitchell Stiles never married. Somewhere in far West.

George Washington Beall. Minerva Ford Beall.

George Beall Wilson and Margaret B. Wilson.

David Stiles' Sons and Their Children.

CHARLES "VALLEY" STILES.

Charles "Valley" Stiles was born 1845, married —— Neff. Issue :

Kirby Stiles.
Ben P. Stiles.
Mattie L. Stiles.
Sudie Stiles.

THOMAS STILES.

Thomas Stiles married Addie Godbey. Issue :

Stella Stiles, d. young.
Guy Stiles, b. 1889.

WILLIAM STILES.

William Stiles married —— Harnett. Issue :

David H. Stiles.
John Thomas Stiles.
Edward Stiles.
Jacob Stiles.
Oscar Lee Stiles.
Fannie C. Stiles.
Nellie M. Stiles.
Lewis Allen Stiles.

Ogden W. Stiles' Grandchildren. See page 12.

REV. SAM P. STILES.

Rev. Sam P. Stiles married Annie Huston. Issue :

Wm. Huston Stiles,	b. 1872,	mar. M. B. Stewart.
Elizabeth Phillips Stiles,	" 1875,	" Edward Palmer.
Lewis Ogden Stiles,	" 1879.	
Alfred Nall Stiles.	" 1884,	d. 1892.

Wm. Huston Stiles' son.

Harlan Chamney Stiles, b. 1894.

LEWIS KITCHELL STILES.

Lewis Kitchell Stiles married Kate Huston. Issue:

Lula Wilson Stiles, b. 1876.
Sam Phillips Stiles, " 1879.
Wm. Davis Stiles, " 1890.

JOHN B. STILES.

John B. Stiles married Sallie Beam. Issue:

Wm. Ogden Stiles, b. 1886.

BEN P. STILES.

Ben P. Stiles married Lena Elliott. See page 13. Issue:

Edna B. Stiles, b. 1890.
Susan A. Stiles, " 1893.

HUGH D. STILES.

Hugh D. Stiles married Woodie Crume. See page 13. Issue:

Ogden Willett Stiles, b. 1895.

Kitchell M. Stiles' Grandchildren. See page 11.

LEWIS OGDEN STILES.

Lewis Ogden Stiles married Nannie Chenault. Issue:

Carrie Stiles.
Stephen Kitchell Stiles.
Lewis Ogden Stiles.
Edna Stiles.

La Fayette Stiles.

THIRD SECTION.

Old Family Letters.

I submit a number of family letters for the reader.—Author.

New Jersey, Morris Co., Randolph.
Februrary 13, 1812.

Dear Nephew (Lewis Stiles):

I would have to prove Grace Homer had separate estate if I made my money. Ask David (Stiles) about that, the debt is honest and just (business).

We are all well at present, hoping to you the same. I remain your affectionate uncle till death.

Moses Hurd.

N. B.—I will write your father and mother soon. Remember our love to them. Munson's (Ezekiel) family is well and desire us to give you their love.

Moses and Mary (Stiles) Hurd.

Natchez, Miss., 24 July, 1812.

Dear Lewis (Stiles):

I am at a loss for some apology sufficient for not writing sooner, be assured it is not for want of respect, it is a hurry of business. The market dull, bacon seven to eight cents, whisky forty-two to forty-five cents per gallon. Please let me hear from you, how you and your gal are getting along, and all the news. I am the same two and a penny. My very best respects to Miss Eunice and Miss Densy and to Miss R—.

I should be glad to have the honor of delivering the message myself. Wishing you long to live and well to do is the wish of

Joe Maxwell.

This man married Eunice (above) in 1814.

Rockaway, N. J., 25 March, 1813.

Lewis Stiles, Honored Cousin :

Father (James) has been to Vermont, went to see your Uncle Jacob Stiles, he and his wife were well, and your Uncle (Jonathan) Ball's family were well.

I need not relate the shameful disaster of Hull, which branded our arms with almost irrecoverable stigma, and no doubt turned the fate of war against us. The battle of Frenchtown, near the River Raisin, had not reached you when I wrote. That was sufficient to raise the indignation of every patriotic mind, the inhuman butchery of our maimed and bleeding soldiers not equalled in the annals of history. I am in hopes the scale will turn the ensuing campaign. Recruiting goes on briskly, so many enlisted in Morris County there is scarcely hands enough to carry on the iron works, which makes wages high. Am in hopes we shall have 50,000 men on the lines by May 1st (1813) ; that is thought a sufficient number for the invasion of Canada. Gen. Dearbon is now at Sackett's Harbor with about 7,000 men ; he will make an attack soon as he can ; he recruited at Plattsburgh, Vt., last winter (1812). Better times for the farmer were never known, wheat is $2.00 to $2.50 per bushel. Hibernia furnace furnishes us a market. The gentlemen that built it overshot themselves and broke flat. Nathan Parrott slipped off last spring and has not been heard

Rebecca Eltengy Pence.

of since. Charles M. Graham, who owns the copperas works, has bought it.

I have been to Newburgh and brought Eliza (Kitchell) home, left Charity there. I am sorry to inform you Uncle Gardner (Thomas) is no more. He died 7th of March (1813), after being confined to his bed about five months. He was never well after the War (Revolutionary). Charles (K.) Gardner has been appointed Captain in the Artillery; last winter he was in New York and acted as Brigadier and aid to Gen. Armstrong; his pay is $96 per month.

I shall be of age 24th of October, and you may expect to see me in that country. Father and mother send greatest regards to all.

Your affectionate cousin,
Mathias Kitchell.

Rockaway, 13th May, 1814.
Dear Lewis (Stiles):

I have looked in vain, etc.

Uncle Joseph (Kitchell) has come out the little end of the horn, also has John Allen. They are at Sackett's Harbor with Uncle Lewis. I went to school at Newburgh last winter, boarded with Aunt Sarah (Gardner). She will quit keeping tavern when she can sell. Charles (K. Gardner) is a Major in 23d Regiment; he wintered at French Mills.

Mr. Graham has sold the copperas works near Hibernia for $42,000, the buyers seem clever men.

Charles is much pleased with his situation, he wrote me that he delighted to be in an engagement. He was gratified to the fullest extent, as he was in the warm-

est of the battle last fall when they attempted to ascend the St. Lawrence River, which was a severe one, yet he was not injured. I have a sore finger and will quit (8 pages). Your cousin,
        Mathias Kitchell.

     Rockaway, N. J., Aug. 3, 1815.
Dear Cousin :
 I have just made my arrival after 21 days. I shall sell the Cooley farm where Uncle Joseph lived and the blacksmith shop. I talk of going to Vermont, if I do, I shall run out your land in lots. Father and mother, Eliza and Charity join me in much love to you all.
      Your cousin,
        Mathias Kitchell.

    Morristown, N. J., April 15, 1815.
Dear Cousin (Lewis Stiles):
 I have been to P. O. every mail for a month, in vain. At last begun to think you had left me to my destruction. I got the $50, hope you will soon collect the other, for nothing but money will make the mare go here.

 I congratulate Rhoda (Stiles) and Griffin (Willett) on their marriage, and mourn that I can not pay Charles (Stiles) a similar compliment. But I shall see you all soon. Father (Darius) thanks you for his letter.   Yours with esteem,
       Isaac Ford Pierson.

      Morristown, Jan. 30, 1818.
Dear Cousin :
 I reached home the 21st, after a 27 days' journey. Father (Darius) thinks of moving out, but it is so very

Martin Vanburen Stiles.

far. Mathias has commenced to keep a little store in Dover. No one to oppose him, he will likely do well. He has settled in Jersey for life. Since I left mother (Eunice) has had an ill turn and she hardly survived. Uncle Joseph has started for Vermont. C. K. Gardner has an heir, they live in New York and Aunt Julia Ann lives with them.   Your cousin,
I. F. Pierson.

Saratoga, N. Y., Nov. 11, 1825.
Dearest Cousin :

By John Pierson, I received your letter with much pleasure indeed. I am here in search of health, will go into other States. They are building a canal from Delaware to Patterson, which passes between Rockaway and our home. I visited the children of Uncle Demas and Lewis Kitchell. Uncle Demas left two daughters, both are married well ; Huta, oldest, married Dr. Doty ; Hannah also married well. Uncle Lewis' widow married Mr. Crane, a wealthy farmer. Mahlon Munson married Henry Parsons' daughter, who is rich. Betsey married a man in Morristown I don't know. Jacob and Munson Hurd are both married, they each married a daughter of Peter Hoagland. Nancy Hurd married Andrew Baker, and has done well. I wish to be remembered to all.

Very affectionately,
Mathias Kitchell.

Morristown, Nov. 17, 1825.
Dear Cousin (Lewis Stiles):

I got home in twenty days after I left you. I find Joseph in bad health, no chance of his ever being any better. Mother (Eunice) is bad off, in all probability will not be with us long. The rest of us all well. The canal comes through our place, there are now 500 hands at work. Uncle (James) Kitchell's family are well; Eliza (Farrand) has four children, Charity (Ford) has four, Uncle Ford has four, none married.

Grandmother and family are about as usual. Ebenezer has lost his wife, left with three small children. Ezekiel Munson has had a stroke of palsy, is bad off. Your Uncle (Moses) Hurd's family are well. I have just come from New York and find C. K. Gardner's folks all well. Julia Ann is not married.

Your sincere friend and cousin,
John K. Pierson.

June 30, 1826.
Dear Uncle (David Stiles):

I hope to give you an account of our family. Eliza has married Samuel Farrand; has four children, Mary Smith, Hannah Day, Eliza Morton and Ebenezer. I have been married nine years the third of July; have four children, Eveline, Azel Kitchell, Edward Gould and Sarah Elizabeth. Uncle Ford has —— children, but one boy, who bears the name of Abraham Ford; none of girls yet married. Aunt Eunice (Pierson) has lost Joseph, died in February. Cyrus Kitchell lives with grandma and the girls. Ebenezer is left with three small children, the eldest not five till September. Nancy and Rebecca have taken the children to grandma's. Ebenezer is blacksmithing at Whippany. Moses Hurd is well, his wife is very delicate; none of the girls married. Jacob and Munson married daugh-

Charity Kitchell Ford.

ters of Peter Hoagland. Jacob has two children. Betsey Munson has married Mr. Pruder. Aunt Munson is quite low, can not last long. Father and Aunt Julia Ann (Gardner) talk of coming to see you, but their ages will not permit of such a journey. Aunt Phebe Kendall is a widow. She is on a visit to Uncle Ford's.

Father and mother, Aunt Gardner and Julia, Aunt Pierson, Uncle Ford, Aunt Betsey and the girls join me in much love to you all.

Affectionately, your niece,
Charity H. Ford.

P. S.—Brother Charles (Gardner) married nine years ago to Eliza McLean; have five children, eldest is John McLean, after his grandfather; Emma Kitchell, Jacob Brown and Charles Thomas. They make Washington their home.   Julia Ann Gardner.

Morristown, N. J., Jan. 29, 1829.

Dear Uncle and Aunt (David Stiles and wife):

I have been depending on John to write, so I will now. I received a letter from Cousin Lewis (Stiles) by John, in which he blames me severely for taking up my abode in New Jersey—"the poor poverty-struck New Jersey." He wonders that I turn my back on promising prospects of the "West" for the "poor deplorable soil of New Jersey." I would come to you but could not leave my unfortunate old father and mother and brother for sake of gain. To have left them would have been to me a source of eternal remorse of conscience. My father on my return I found in the last stages of his existence, and within less than one year we were called on to perform the last act of friendship. My brother lingered a little while longer and he took his leave of us forever. Mother had no prospect of surviving them, but contrary to all expectations, still survives. It has been a dark day for us, but we have stood up bravely, and mother is fast improving and our prospects brightening.

Ezekiel Munson's wife (Rhoda Stiles) died last winter of a lingering disease, and in the fall he was called to follow her. Grandma Kitchell (Sarah Ford) died 9th of this month of old age. She lived out all her days of comfort. Samuel Kitchell (James' son) has been severely afflicted for four or five months. Cyrus (Kitchell) married to a young wife (Mary), daughter of Aher Fairchild. Ebenezer has his second wife and lives at Whippany. Nancy and Rebecca live at old homestead. Charles K. Gardner has bought property in Washington and is employed in P. O. Department at $1,600 a year. He makes politics his business and is a very smart man. As he has been an advocate of Gen. Jackson he will be promoted. I forgot to say John has a boy nine months old, and a fine boy he is.

Love to all.   Your nephew,

I. F. Pierson.

NOTE.—No wonder this man died possessed of a fortune; his fidelity to his parents was without limit.   AUTHOR.

Lebanon, Ky., March 8, 1833.
Dear Uncle (James Kitchell):

I received your letter by Mr. Grundy, greatly pleased to hear from you. Father (David Stiles) has bad health, has not been to see me for three years.

Dr. John C. Maxwell.

We are all married except Abraham (Stiles). Densy (Phillips) is left a widow with five small children. My second son (J. C. Maxwell) is now in college at Danville, Ky. He will finish at Princeton and enter the ministry. Give my affectionate love to Charity and Eliza (Kitchell). I shall ever remember the pleasant hours spent with them. My love to all.

Your affectionate niece,
Eunice (Stiles) Maxwell.

Bridport, Vt., Nov. 1, 1833.
Dear Brother (David Stiles):

I received your letter, first one since you left N. J. I would have written but did not know where to write. Betsey's (Losey) health is good for one of here age. I live on the farm I bought when I came here from N. J. I am doing well, am nearly 66 years old and can not expect to live a great while longer. We shall not probably ever meet here together in this world, but, O, dear brother, may we all be prepared to meet in the world to come. We wish you to write often, it is a source of great pleasure to hear from you. Tell your children to write me and come make me a visit.

Write to and remember your affectionate brother,
Jacob Stiles.

Washington, 16 February, 1833.
My Dear Cousin:

I intended before this to have written you fully, but a continued pressure of business at this season seems unrelenting. I was very happy to hear from you, and gave my mother (Sarah Kitchell) your letter. (Then follows P. O. matters, etc.

The "Nullifiers" appear to have backed out, which I did not expect of the men engaged. Calhoun seems to have accepted the first proposition of compromise made by your son of Kentucky (Clay), though it gives very slowly, but too much in the long run, unless it is designed to deceive them before nine years' expire. I doubt if Aunt Stiles (Elizabeth Kitchell) would remember me, but let me be made known to your father and mother and all my cousins.

Yours truly and affectionately,
C. K. Gardner.

Rockaway, N. J., March 24, 1837.

Dear Cousin (Lewis Stiles):

I married a granddaughter of Benj. Beach, Esq., the one you sold your Horse Pond farm to, a daughter of Capt. S. S. Beach. I have two children, Charles Henry, and a girl, Caroline Beach. Charity (Ford) has seven children, one married to Col. Ford Kitchell, who lives near me; they have three children. Samuel Farrand has become wealthy. I was at your old homestead farm (Horse Pond). There is none of your old neighbors left. Your cousin,

Mathias Kitchell.

Stanhope, N. J., May 31, 1840.

Cousin Lewis (Stiles):

I received your letter of February last giving the mournful news of the death of Uncle David (Stiles). It is melancholy to see our aged friends depart forever; it reminds us in language well understood that yet a little while and we too must follow and leave all things we hold dear. These are solemn reflections. James Kitchell is in good health and smart as he was ten years ago, he is really an old patriarch (81), worthy of honor and respect. Mathias will get rich. Remember us affectionately to all. Let us correspond.

Your cousin,
Isaac F. Pierson.

NOTE.—This letter covered eight pages.

Rockaway, N. J., Feb. 26, 1847.

Dear Cousin :

This will inform you of the death of my father and Ford Kitchell, they died near the same time, with a number of my wife's (Caroline Beach) relatives. Uncle Ford Kitchell's son lives on his old farm. My stepmother and her son live on father's old farm. Myself and Samuel Farrand are their trustees. Aunt Eunice Pierson boards with Charity at Dover. She liked to have burned up in the house in Pennsylvania. Isaac Pierson has 22,000 acres in Pennsylvania, brings lumber down the canal. Rockaway has six stores, two taverns, lot 50 feet front 100 feet deep sell for $100 —on a boom. The Canal Company paid me $1,500 after a long contest.

The lowering of the tariff, as I was in the iron business, like to have ruined me. It has gone down from $85 and $90 a ton to about $50, and had I not had a large farm to depend on, would have broke me up. I regret that any of the Old Kitchell stock, who were such firm Whigs in the revolution and firm Jefferson Democrats, should belong to the rotten Democracy of this day, whose only virtue consists in propagation of falsehoods and adhering to the same as though they were true, thereby duping honest men. I wonder if your sensibilities are not shocked at this Democratic government. I only say there is not one of the old stock in this county that belongs to that party. I served the past two years in our Legislature, but can not go back.

Mahlon Munson owns the "Old Stiles farm," and is well off. I saw Charles in Washington not long ago, he is well.   Your cousin,

Mathias Kitchell.

Washington, 3d June, 1847.
Dear Cousin :

I have just received your letter in regard to balance due as mail contractor, etc.

I am glad you have written me, for I can now, though so late, renew our intercourse which has been suspended since we were boys. I often hear from you through Mr. Wickliffe (Congressman) and should be glad to hear more of your family and your brothers' families. I have five sons and three daughters (having lost one in family). The only one married is my eldest daughter, Emma Kitchell, to Alex. Mouton (who shortly afterwards was elected Governor of Louisiana). My eldest son, John, who studied law in New York, is principal clerk in my post-office here. My next son, Jacob Brown, is a graduate in medicine, and during my depression and removal from office by the Whigs, set up an apothecary store which he continues on Capital Hill. Of my third son, Franklin, he is a Second Lieutenant in Seventh Regiment, hav-

Mathias Day Kitchell.

ing graduated at West Point in 1843, and has been in Mexico from the first movement of the regiment to Corpus Christi to the present time, where I suppose he is in Mexico City in Twigg's division. I sent you last week a report of the storming of Cerro Gordo, at which he was so lucky as to command a company and to be detached to maintain a position of observation. He was in Gen. Worth's division at the storming of Monterey, as you will find in Worth's report that he gave him great distinction for his gallantry there, and the government made him a brevet First Lieutenant. The rest of my children are at home.

I hope you will choose a Democrat from your district in the next Congress, as it will be very closely divided. There is no telling what will be the state of parties when the war with Mexico draws to a close. So much depends on that conclusion and on the wants which are connected with the war. The Whigs (as they call themselves) it appears to me are going to make Gen. Scott their candidate for President; they are afraid to trust "Old Rough and Ready," he will be too strict a constructionist for them, and too firm to be swayed to their purpose.

I shall be glad to hear from you and all about Uncle Stiles' family. I am, very sincerely,

Your friend and cousin,

C. K. Gardner.

NOTE.—This man was then Postmaster General, United States of America.—AUTHOR.

Johnson Co., Mo., Aug. 7, 1847.

Dear Brother:

This is the best country in the world, tell John and

Abraham to come. Proc. Phillips is prospecting, it will be a great day's work for him if he buys. You asked about my children, I have only one of the last set, James Riley. My wife and children join me in sending you much love. Come and see me.

Your brother,
Demas Stiles.

On July 21, 1853, this man says, "my two sons, David and Henry, left last May for California to dig gold."

Bridport, Vt., Jan. 29, 1848.

Yours of Dec. 4 is before me. You are not right, my father married your Aunt Sally's (Losey) daughter. He died 1825. Mother is living, has three children living, myself, brother and sister. My mother has one brother, Herman Losey, who resides in Willoughby, O. Your Aunt Sally (Stiles) Ball died December, 1847. There are four heirs in Ball family, William, David, Alexander, Lucinda living, and Moses dead. You have no uncles or aunts living of Stiles name here. The cause of Uncle and Aunt (Jacob) Stiles' death were the infirmities of old age and the extreme warm weather. Uncle had been a cripple for a number of years before his death and aunt perfectly blind for six years.

Charles C. Pettibone.

Dover, N. J., Sept. 2, 1848.

Dear Cousin :

I received your letter yesterday, glad indeed to hear from all, etc.

I married Henry Parsons' daughter, Eunice, have seven children, the oldest twenty-four, youngest eight.

Henrietta, Mahlon, Charles, Rhoda, Emeline, Mary and Robert. Polly's (Hurd) husband is living. Their son came from Mexico six weeks ago from the war. Jonathan Ball sold his interest in Jacob's (Stiles) estate to Stiles Pettibone.

Present my love to all my cousins.

Yours Truly,

Mahlon Munson.

To Capt. Lewis Stiles.

FOURTH DIVISION.

Kindred of the Kentucky Stiles.

David Stiles left in New Jersey and Vermont four sisters :

ELIZABETH STILES.

Elizabeth Stiles, born 1761, died 1841, married Abraham Losey. Issue :

Herman Losey (went to Willoughby, O., in early days).
Sally Losey, b 1787, d 1865, mar Isaac Pettibone.

Isaac and Sally Pettibone's children :

Betsey Emeline Pettibone, b 1808, d 1877, mar C. A. Wicker.
Charles Case Pettibone, " 1810, " 1883, " Mahitable Gale.
Edwin Stiles Pettibone, " 1815, " 1877, " Marion Pease.
Nancy Cordelia Pettibone, " 1818, " 1842.

Charles C. Pettibone's children :

Helen C. Pettibone.
Julia E. Pettibone.
Nancy A. Pettibone.
George I. Pettibone.

Stiles Pettibone's children :

Edwin L. Pettibone.
Francis E. Pettibone.
Florence E. Pettibone.
Charles B. Pettibone.
Wilbur Losey Pettibone.

Jacob Stiles Hurd.

SALLIE STILES.

Sallie Stiles, born —, died 1847, married Jonathan Ball. Issue :

William, David Stiles, Alexander, Lucinda and Moses Ball. (No information from these or their descendants.)

MARY STILES.

Mary Stiles, born —, died 1830 or '31, married Moses Hurd. Issue :

Jacob Stiles Hurd,	mar Mary Hoagland in 1823.
Ezekiel Munson Hurd,	" Phebe Hoagland.
Nancy Hurd,	" Andrew Baker.
Moses Hurd,	" Mary Pregnon.
Malinda Hurd, b 1805,	" Manning Rutan. See photo.
Elizabeth Hurd,	Never married.
Maria Hurd,	" Thomas Kirkpatrick.
Harriet Hurd,	" E. Peck.

Jacob S. Hurd's children :

Elizabeth Ann Hurd,	Never married (dead).
Emma Caroline Hurd,	mar Jacob VanDeventer.
John Ward Hurd,	" (1) Hawley, (2) King.

Munson Hurd's children :

Mary Hurd,	mar Edward Benjamin.
William Hurd.	
Edward Hurd.	
Andrew D. Hurd.	
Cornelia Hurd,	" Simon D. Rose.

Nancy Hurd married Andrew Baker. Issue :

Emily Baker,	mar Henry Bysam.
Jeremiah Baker,	" Salmon.
Adeline Baker,	" Thomas Post.
Louisa M. Baker,	" Jas. R. Beemer.
Elizabeth Ann Baker,	" David Jardine.
Adolphus Baker,	" (1) Kanorose, (2)——
Augustus Baker,	" ——

Moses Hurd, Jr.'s, children :

Harriet Hurd.
Mary Lib. Hurd,   mar Peter VanDerhoof.
Frank Hurd (dead).
Minnie Hurd,   " Thomas Tone.

Malinda Hurd married Manning Rutan. Now living at Greenville, Mich., aged ninety-one years. See photo. Issue :

Eugene Rutan.

Maria Hurd married Thomas Kirkpatrick. Issue :

Jacob H. Kirkpatrick,   mar Fanny Swinnerton.
Manning Kirkpatrick.
Eugene Kirkpatrick,   " Jennie Skinner.
Amity Kirkpatrick,   " ——

Harriet Hurd married E. Peck. Issue :

Josephine Peck.
Emogene Peck.
Solon Peck.

RHODA STILES.

Rhoda Stiles, born —, died 1828, married Ezekiel Munson. Issue :

Mahlon Munson,   mar Eunice Parsons.
Polly Munson,   " Hurd.
Elizabeth Munson.   " Pruden.

Mahlon Munson's children :

Harriet Munson,	b 1824,		mar Tuttle.	
Robert H. Munson,	" 1826,		" Siphia Briant.	
Mahlon O. Munson,	" 1828,		" Phebe A. Coe.	
Charles H. Munson,	" 1830,		" Margaret Shaw.	
Rhoda Munson,	" 1833,	d 1869,	" Charles M. Tunis.	
Sarah E. Munson,	" 1835,		" M. V. B. Searing.	
Mary E. Munson,	" 1837,	" 1858,	" Nelson Young.	

Malinda Hurd Rutan.
Aged 92, resides at Greenville, Mich.

Polly Munson married Hurd.   Issue:

Emeline M. Hurd,   mar Fales.
Adia Hurd.
Amanda Hurd.

Elizabeth Munson married Pruden.   Issue:

Elizabeth Pruden,   mar Crane.

ABRAHAM KITCHELL'S FAMILY.

David Stiles' wife was Elizabeth Kitchell, as stated before, daughter of Abraham and Sarah Ford Kitchell.

A complete list of Abraham Kitchell's family is as follows:

James Kitchell,	b 1759,	d 1842,	mar Hannah Day.
Sarah Kitchell,	" 1761,	" 1839,	" Thomas Gardner.
Elizabeth Kitchell,"	1764,	" 1831,	" David Stiles.
Eunice Kitchell,	" 1766,	" 1863,	" Darius Pierson.
Ford Kitchell,	" 1770,	" 1842,	" Elizabeth McCarty.
Demas Kitchell,	" 1772.		
Lewis Kitchell,	" 1775,	" 1876.	

Abraham Kitchell married [2] Rebecca Farrand.   Issue:

Lewis Kitchell,	b 1778,	d 1814,	mar Mary Compton.
Joseph Kitchell,	" 1779,	" 1847,	" Minter.
Abraham Kitchell,	" 1781,	" ——	
Charity Kitchell,	" 1782,		" John Allen.
Nancy Kitchell,	" 1785,	" 1867,	Never married.
Cyrus Kitchell,	" 1787,		" Mary Fairchild.
Ebenezer, } Rebecca, }	" 1787,	" young.	
Rebecca Kitchell,	" 1792,	" 1868,	" Demas Badgely.
Ebenezer Kitchell,	" 1794,		" Joanna Tuttle.

Only a few of these people or their descendants are known to Kentucky Stiles. By the reading of the family letters in my possession I make out this list.

James and Hannah Days Kitchell's children:

Azell Kitchell,	b 1790,	d 1809 (accident).	
Mathias Days Kitchell,	" 1792,	" 1857,	m Caroline Beach.
Eliza Thompson Kitchell,	" 1795,	" 1867,	" Sam'l Farrand.
Charity H. Kitchell,	" 1798,	" 1875,	" James Ford.

Mathias Kitchell's children:

Charles Henry Kitchell,	b 1835,		m Margaret Hazzard.
Caroline Beach Kitchell,	" 1836,	d 1838.	
Mathias Days Kitchell,	" 1838,		" Amsa Doughty.
Henrietta S. Kitchell,	" 1839,		" Silas M. Cowles.
James T. Kitchell,	" ——		" Irene Matthews.
Horace Beach Kitchell,	" 1843,		" Mrs. Jeon Lathom.
Frank Thompson Kitchell	" 1845,	" 1847.	
Walter Kitchell,	" 1849,	" ——	

Charity (Kitchell) Ford's children:

Eveline Ford,	b 1818.		
Azel Kitchell Ford,	" 1820,	d 1884.	
Edward Gould Ford,	" 1823,		m Phebe Lanback.
Sarah Elizabeth Ford,	" 1825,		" J. Munson Beach.
Harriet Ford,	" 1827,		" J. E. Cutler.
Nancy Caroline Ford,	" 1830,		" Wm. T. Round.
Mary Conger Ford,	" 1835.		
Ellen L. Ford,	" 1838,	" 1887.	
Hannah Maria Ford,	" 1840,		" Abner D. Thurber.

Elizabeth (Kitchell) Farrand's children:

Mary Smith Farrand,	b 1817,		m James Harry Ball.
Hannah Day Farrand,	" 1819.		
Eliza Morton Farrand,	" 1822,		" Abr. Ford Kitchell.
Susan Smith Farrand,	" 1829,		" Benjamin B. Green.
Nancy Benedict Farrand	" 1831,		" James H. Quinby.
Margaret J. Farrand,	" 1835,	d 1872,	" Charles F. Ogden.
Phenias Farrand,	" 1838,		" (1) Mary Darling, (2) Susan Ogden.

Mahlon Munson.

Sarah Kitchell married Thomas Gardner. Issue :

Charles Kitchell Gardner, b 1787, d 1869, P. M. Gen., U. S. A.
Julia Ann Gardner, " 1790, " 1859, never married.

Charles K. Gardner married Eliza McLean. Issue :

Emma Kitchell Gardner,	b 1819,		m Alex. Mouton, U. S. Senator.
John McLean Gardner,	" 1817,	d ——	Bachelor.
Jacob Brown Gardner,	" 1821,	" ——	" Rosa M. Manning.
Franklin Gardner,	" 1823,	" 1873,	" M. C. Mouton.
Charles Thomas Gardner	(died young).		
Sarah A. McL. Gardner,			" John J. Almy, Admiral U. S. N.
Charles Thomas Gardner,"	——	" ——,	" Anna Wilson.
George Clinton Gardner,	.		" Mary F. Brodhead.
Alida Armstrong Gardner,			" John J. Almy (2 m).

Eunice Kitchell married Darius Pierson. Issue :

Isaac F. Pierson,	b 1795,	d 1872,	Bachelor.
John K. Pierson,	" 1796,	" 1869,	m Catherine Ford.
Joseph C. Pierson,	" 1798,	" 1826.	
Rhoda Pierson	(died young).		

John K. Pierson's children :

Rhoda W. Pierson,	b 1830.
Isaac F. Pierson,	" 1832. (In New York.)
Wm. M. Pierson,	" 1834.
Charles C. Pierson,	" 1836.
Sarah E. Pierson,	" 1838.

Miscellaneous.

REGRET the valuable book, "The Stiles Family in America and England," by Henry Reed Stiles, No. 113 William St., New York City, had not reached me before this work (in most part) had gone to press. His work gives full history of the Connecticut Family, settlers at Windsor, Conn., in 1636, from which, through its branches, our Kentucky and Missouri Families of the name are descended.

IT is suggested that Thomas Stiles (David's father) had eight children. An old deed of record in Morristown, N. J., mentions eight. Two sons, James and John, were young at their father's death, and their mother soon married —— Goble, and these two sons were raised by Goble and wife. From family tradition I believe this correct. The descendants of these live in Philadelphia and they are numerous.

ISAAC F. PIERSON was in Kentucky the last time in October, 1867. At one time (1819) he and Jonathan Ford bought up a large territory of land in Kentucky, but it proven to be of little value as a speculation.

IN 1828 Isaac F. Pierson was elected Coroner of Morris County, N. J., "but it will be of little use to me."

IN 1819 Charles K. Gardner took charge of the New York State Arsenal.

THE Kentucky Stiles were never much litigious, only three civil cases recorded in Kentucky Court of Appeals. No criminal prosecutions ever been recorded where the Commonwealth (State) prosecuted any Stiles. No divorce proceedings have ever been had, or of record, by parties of this name in this State.

THE Kentucky Stiles may feel proud of the fact their earlier ancestors and collateral kinsmen in "Jersey" took active part in defending American Liberty. In examining the Revolutionary War record from New Jersey, I find the following enlistments:

STILES—Daniel, David, Samuel, Moses H., Joseph and Elijah, of Morris County, and Timothy, of Essex County.
Officers—Jonathan Stiles (David's grandfather), express rider; John Stiles, Commissary of Issues.

KITCHELL—James, Abraham, Aaron (a wagoner) and ten others.

FORD—Stephen, manned boat "Mifflin."
Jacob, Jr., Colonel, Jan. 10, 1777. Died at Morristown of pneumonia; buried with military honors by order of Washington.
Chillion, Second Lieutenant, Aug. 10, 1777.
Jonathan (see page 42), and sixteen others.

MUNSON—Mahlon, made Captain Sept 26, 1780 (and others). Mahlon, on page 35, is a grandson.

FARRAND—Samuel, Daniel, James and others.

HOAGLAND—Peter (Jacob and Munson Hurd's father-in-law. See page 25.)

HURD—David, Stephen, Daniel and others.

PIERSON—Abraham, Samuel, Capt. Sec. Reg. "Continental Troops"; Joseph, David, Lieut. in Elmere's Company. See Rev. H. D. Kitchell's genealogy.

OGDEN—Mathias, granted leave to go to Europe.
David, Jonathan, Stephen, wounded at "Second River."

GARDNER—Thomas, was with Gen. Rochambeau's Army. (See account of his death, page 23.)

THE younger generation of this day and time ought to keep fresh in memory these patriotic men, who for liberty marched over frozen ground without a shoe or stocking, often tracing them in the snow and over the frozen earth by the blood from their bleeding feet. No wonder, on page 23, we read that one of these heroes was never well after his service in this war. But relying on the justice of their cause, they pressed forward, crying, "We are fighting for liberty, let us have freedom from oppression for ourselves and our children."

IN 1824 Mathias Kitchell spoke of the celebrated case of Gibbons vs. Ogden (Aaron), known as "The Steamboat Case from New York." It involved the right to navigate the waters by steamboat and carry passengers between Elizabethtown, N. J., and New York City. It was argued by some of the most learned and distinguished jurists of the age.

IN 1828 mention is made of a circular gotten out by some "unscrupulous person" on Gen. Andrew Jackson. There was a picture of six coffins, representing soldiers court-martialed and shot near Mobile in 1815. This circular made a bitter attack on "Old Hickory," but the writer of the letter was a strong admirer and supporter of the General. An interesting account of this circular was recently published in the Louisville Courier-Journal.

IN 1835 Rev. Joseph Clay Stiles was a noted preacher in Central Kentucky.

See Littell's Life of Ben Hardin, also H. R. Stiles' genealogy, pp 680-9.

The children of Lewis Fisk Stiles are as follows (see page 5):

William I. Stiles,	b 1863,	m Ella ——.
Nannie C. Stiles,	" 1865,	" F. V. Porter.

Issue by second wife, M. M. Farmer:

Albert Stiles,	b 1873,	m Mary Whipple.
Clifton T. Stiles,	" 1875.	

Martha M. Stiles (dead).

CHILDREN of Abraham Stiles and Ellen Thomas Stiles (see page 5):

Washington T. Stiles,	b 1852,	m Bettie Kitlinger.
Charles B. Stiles,	" 1854,	" Bettie Morris.
Mary L. Stiles,	" 1856,	" J. R. Beeler.
John Stiles,	" 1862,	" Eva Farmer.
Annie J. Stiles,	" 1864,	" Abe Vancleve.

Emma E. Stiles.
Flora Stiles.

By the kindness of Miss Flora Stiles, I received this information very recently. AUTHOR.

The Willett Family.

The Willett family, married into by the Stiles (Lewis and Charles), came to Kentucky about the time the State was founded, from Maryland. On June 1, 1829, John Schley, whose wife was Mary Willett, wrote to Griffin Willett (or Griffin's father) and called them "Dear Uncle and Aunt." John and Mary (Willett) Schley's children were:

Henry, married ——, had three children.
George, single.
David, married Miss Hoke, of Hartford, Conn.
William, single, a lawyer.
————, married daughter of Gen. Ringgold.
Margaret, married Dr. Goldsborough.
Edward, married Miss Bringle.
John T., married, returned from law schools of Connecticut.
Frederick, aged 15.

Mary Willett's (supra) father is not mentioned. Her brothers and sisters are:

Andrew Willett.
David Willett.
Rachel Willett.
Abraham Willett.
Isaac Willett.
Jacob Willett.
Susan Willett.

The descendants of these were many at that day (1829), and now, no doubt, are extremely numerous in Maryland.

www.ingramcontent.com/pod-product-compliance
Lightning Source LLC
Chambersburg PA
CBHW020730100426
42735CB00038B/1455